I0413887

THE HUGE BOOK OF DANDELIONS

Cool Stuff

You didn't know

Plus, Beautiful

Pictures to Color

as you learn

Created by:

Flower Sniffer and Bunny Kisser
Kai Bantaign'

Lover of all things Nature'

THIS BOOK IS DEDICATED TO

NOAH AND EMILY.

MY REASON FOR LIVING.
MY HEART.
MY HAPPY.

ISBN-13: 978-1533206534

ISBN-10: 1533206538

Medical Disclaimer

They're the most unpopular
plant in the neighborhood
but it wasn't always that way.
Before the invention of lawns
the golden blossoms and
lion-toothed leaves were more
likely to be praised as a
bounty of food, medicine and magic.

The name "dandelion"
comes from
the French
"dent de lion"
or lion's tooth
which refers to
the serrated leaves.

Another folk name
for dandelion is
"swine snort"
which makes me want to
sneeze or giggle
or both.

Dandelions are
just plain fun
In a park or garden it's the
only flower a kid can
pick without getting
into trouble.
A child in a field full of
dandelions will never run out
of things to do

The dandelion
is the only flower
that represents
the 3 celestial
bodies of the
sun, moon
and stars.

The yellow flower is the sun

the puff ball is the moon

and the dispersing seeds

are the stars.

Dandelions are among
the most expensive items
in the grocery store.

The roots are dried
and sold as a no-caffeine
coffee substitute
for $31.75 a pound.

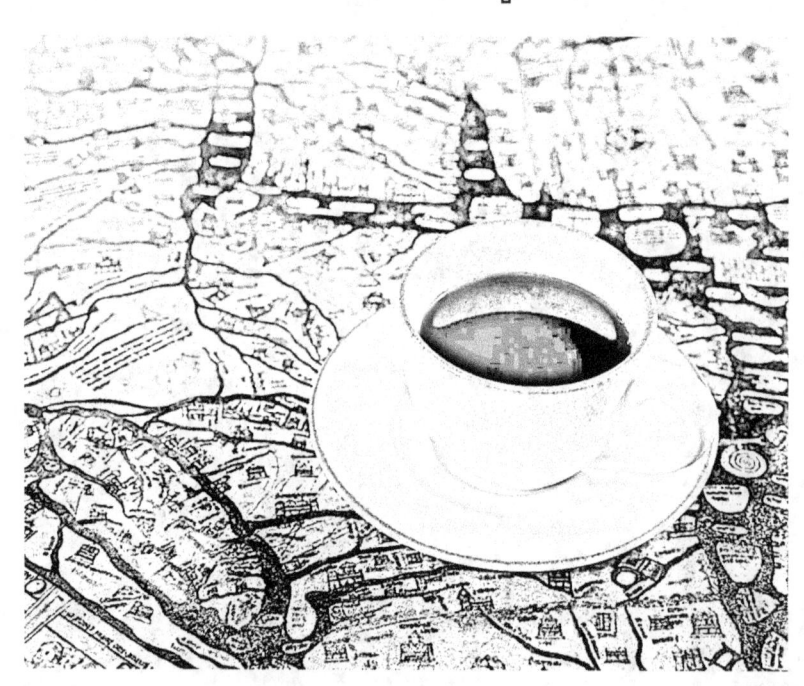

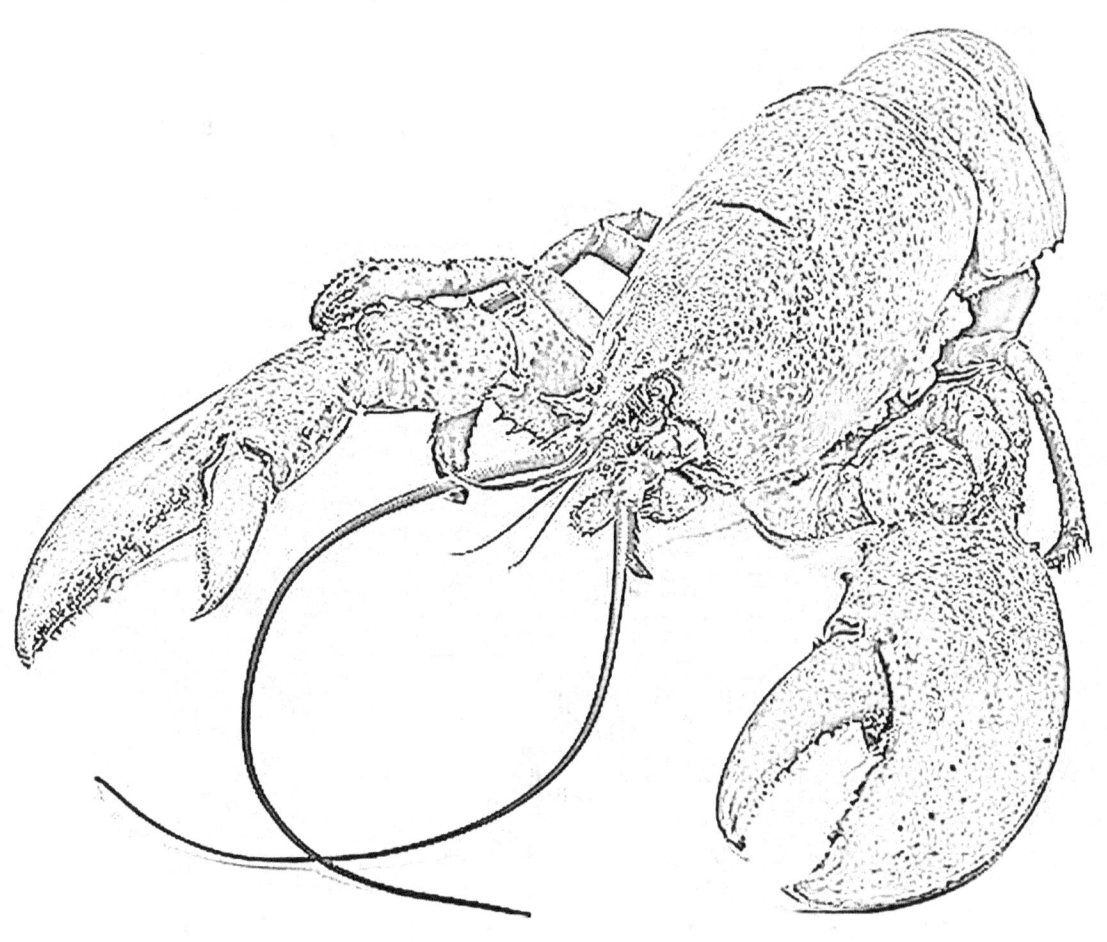

Dandelions out-price prime rib
swordfish and lobster.
They appear in produce
and other sections, and
even at the liquor store.

You can enjoy a complete meal
from salad greens to
dandelion quiche,
followed by
dandelion ice cream,
washed down
with dandelion wine.

If you over-indulge,
a cup of dandelion tea
is the perfect remedy,
as dandelions help the
liver flush hangover-inducing
toxins from the body.

Up until the 1800s
people would pull grass
out of their lawns
to make room for dandelions
and other useful "weeds"
like chickweed,
malva, and chamomile.

The ideal time for
picking dandelion is
the beginning of April.

Dandelion leaves
are great for a salad,
and you can mix them
with eggs and potatoes.

This salad is higher
in vitamins than
tomatoes and spinach.

Fresh dandelion leaves
are very low in calories;
providing just 45
calories per 100 g.

The herb is also a
good source of dietary
fiber and its latex is
a good laxative.
Drinking Dandelion Tea
regularly can help reduce
weight and control cholesterol
levels in the blood.

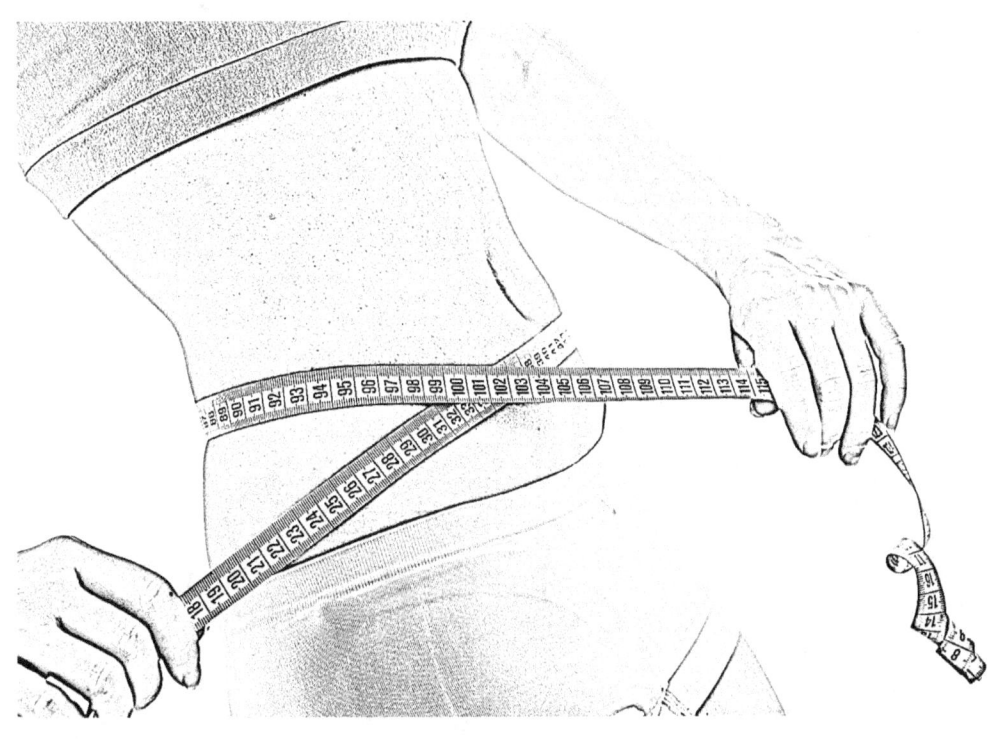

Its a good source of
minerals like potassium, calcium,
manganese, iron, and magnesium.

Potassium helps regulate
heart rate and blood pressure.

Iron is key for red
blood cell production.

Manganese is used by
the body as a co-factor
for the antioxidant enzyme,
superoxide dismutase.

Dandelion herb contains notable nutrients and is a great source of nutrition during winter
This humble backyard
herb provides (%of RDA/100g)-
9% of dietary fiber,
19% of vitamin B-6 (pyridoxine),
20% of Riboflavin,
58% of vitamin C,
338% of vitamin A,
649% of vitamin K,
39% of iron and
19% of calcium.

Its leaves packed with
numerous flavonoids
such as carotene-ß,
carotene-a, lutein,
crypto-xanthin and zea-xanthn.

Carotenes help protect you
from lung and oral cavity cancers.

Zeaxanthin possesses
photo-filtering functions

and may help
protect
the retina from
harmful UV
rays.

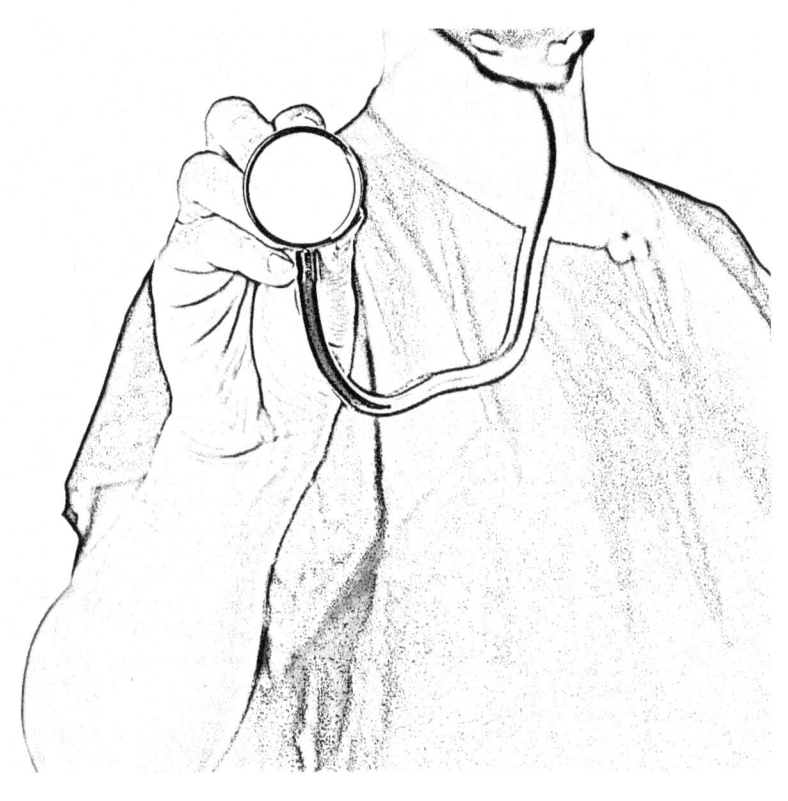

Dandelion root as
well as other plant
parts contains bitter
crystalline compounds
Taraxacin, and an acrid
resin,Taraxacerin.
The root also contains inulin
(not insulin)
and levulin.
Together, these compounds
are responsible for various
therapeutic properties
of the herb.

Dandelion is also rich in many vital vitamins including folic acid, riboflavin, pyridoxine, niacin, vitamin-E and vitamin-C that are essential for optimum health.

Vitamin-C is a powerful natural antioxidant.

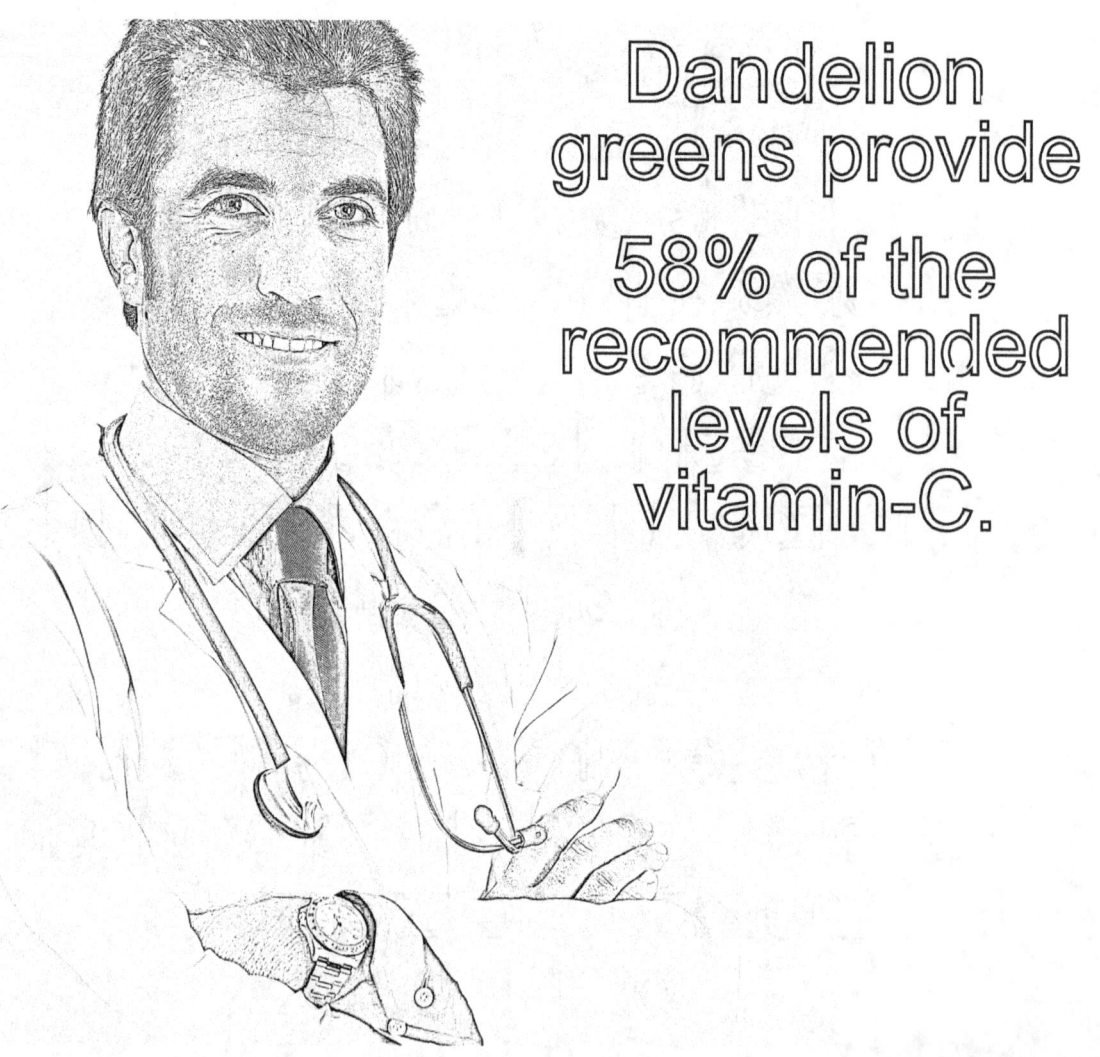

Dandelion greens provide

58% of the recommended levels of vitamin-C.

Dandelion is one of the richest herbal sources of vitamin K.

It provides about 650% of DRI.

Vitamin-K has an important role in bone strengthening by promoting osteotrophic activity in the bones.

It also helps Alzheimer's patients by limiting neuronal damage in the brain.

Dandelions are known
as ruderals or
pioneer plants,
the first to colonize
disturbed land
(like after a wildfire).

FIREFIGHTERS
RULE
BECAUSE

1. They're ready to respond at a moments notice.
2. They're willing to work as volunteers.
3. No one carries a bigger hose.

Dandelion blossoms
have been historically
used to treat warts,
clear skin complexion,
and heal blisters.

The Dandelion has a
yellow-orange flower
that consists of large
number of individual,
miniature flowers
known as ray florets.

These cute little flowers
are photosensitive;
they bloom under the
morning sun and close
in the evening or in
dull, gloomy conditions.

Different types of insects
pollinate dandelion,
not just bees.

The yellow flower turns
into puff ball that is
really a bunch of tiny
fruits called achenes.

Lots of animals such as birds insects and butterflies consume the nectar or seeds of dandelions.

A dandelion seed can travel 5 miles before it finally reaches the ground.

Dandelion is useful in
gardens because it
improves quality of
the soil by increasing
the content of nitrogen
and other minerals.

Dandelion is used often
in Asian cuisine,
as an ingredient of salads and
sandwiches.

The plant was brought
to the US by
the Spanish (New Mexico)
and the German (Pennsylvania)
for use in nutrition.

In Chinese medicine, the dandelion plant has been used for over a thousand years in treating various conditions like diabetes, cancers, as well as bacterial and fungal infections.

Dandelion is popular for its diuretic properties and it increases urine output.

Dandelion greens are on Dr. Mercola's "most highly recommended vegetables" list.

Dandelion Greens
Nutrition Facts
Serving Size:
One cup of raw, chopped
dandelion greens
(about 55 grams)
Amt. Per Serving

Calories	25
Protein	1 g
Fiber	2 g
Carbohydrate	5 mg
Sodium	42 mg

The pollen particles from
dandelions are too large
and sticky to cause
hay fever, and the seed fluffs
are obviously too big to be inhaled;
it's the milky substance inside
the dandelion stem that can
cause irritation.

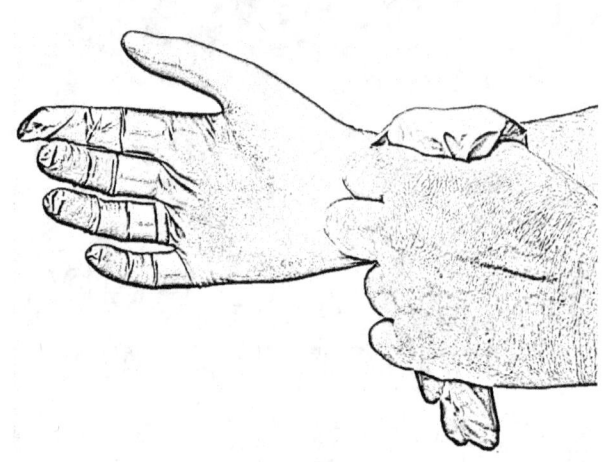

That substance is a latex,
and if you are sensitive to the
manufactured types you
may find yourself irritated by
dandelion latex too.

To begin with, it is
considered a ruderal.
Ruderals are the kinds
of plants that are first to
colonize an area after a
catastrophe.
Most ruderals establish
quickly but easily succumb
to competition from
slower-growing plants.
Dandelions are built to last, though.

Long, Low-to-the-ground leaves

shade the soil around them,
preventing new plants from

sprouting.

They thwart the

competition

before it even

has a chance.

Exotics.
Dandelions are Exotics
which is to say,
they are not native to
North America.

Vitamin A is an important
fat-soluble vitamin and
anti-oxidant, required for
maintaining healthy mucus
membranes and skin and vision.
Fresh dandelion leaves carry
10,161 IU of vitamin-A per 100 g
(about 338% of daily-recommended
intake), one of the highest sources
of vitamin-A among culinary herbs.

Cultivating dandelions.
Dandelion leaves are a common
component of mesclun mix salad,
a very popular and
pricey meal option.

Here's a bizarre twist:

where they're raised as a
cash crop (Like Brazil)
one can find work weeding
around the dandelions.

Dandelion leaves, which are responsible for the plants energy and regeneration grow very close to the ground where lawn mowers don't harm them.
Dandelions are perennial so they'll be back regardless of whether they flower, and if they put all their energy into developing roots and leaves instead of seeds, they'll be that much stronger
The plants adapt quite readily by blooming below the mower blade height.

Native Americans boiled
the herb to make a tea
to treat swelling,
various skin conditions,
kidney disease,
and indigestion.

Chinese physicians
used dandelion extensively
particularly to treat
breast disorders
digestive upset
and appendicitis.

European herbalists added
the herb to preparations
used in the treatment of boils,
fever, eye disease,
digestive ailments
and diabetes.

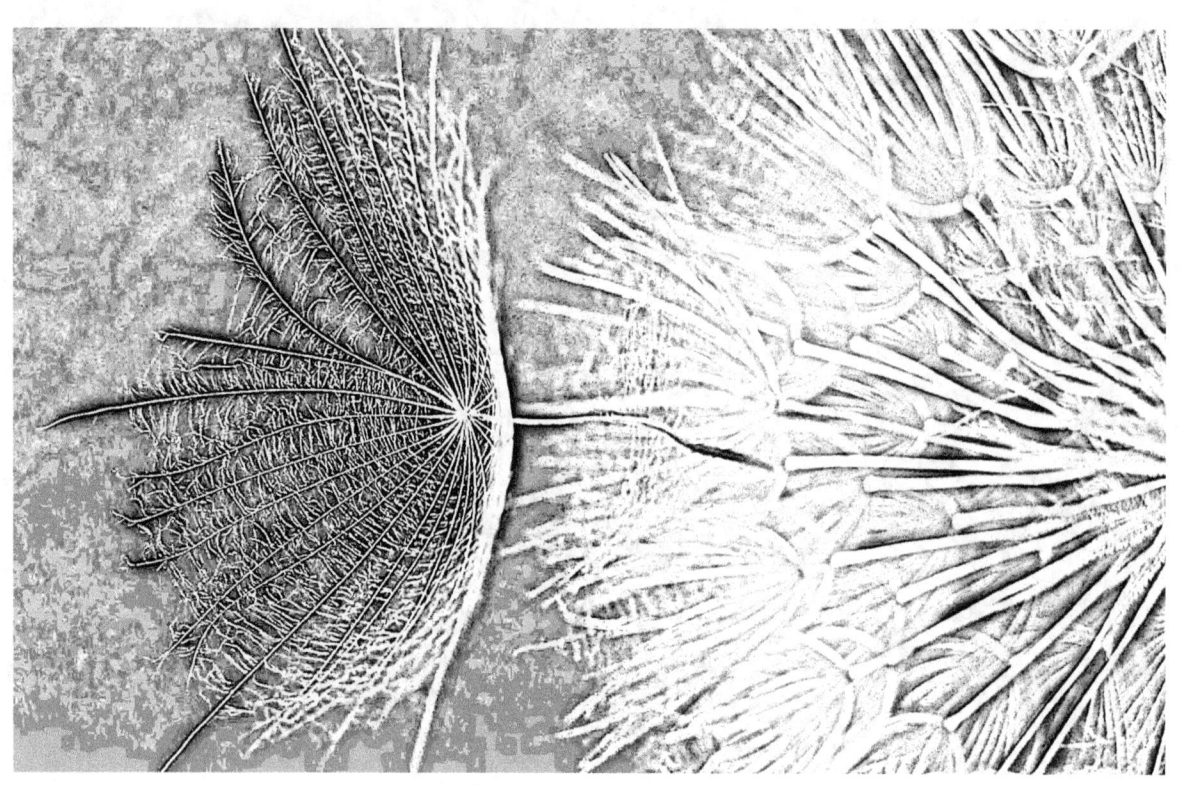

The average American
recognizes
fewer than five plants that
grow in their area.
Dandelions are most likely
one of those familiar plants.

Dandelions have sunk their roots deep into history.

They were well known to ancient Egyptians, Greeks and Romans, and have been used in Chinese traditional medicine for over a thousand years.

In the terrifying New World
the cheerful dandelion would
have been a sweet
reminder of home.

In Japan, whole horticultural
societies formed to enjoy
the beauty of dandelions
and to develop exciting
new varieties for gardeners.

For millennia, dandelion tonics
have been used to
help the body's filter, the liver,
remove toxins from
the bloodstream.

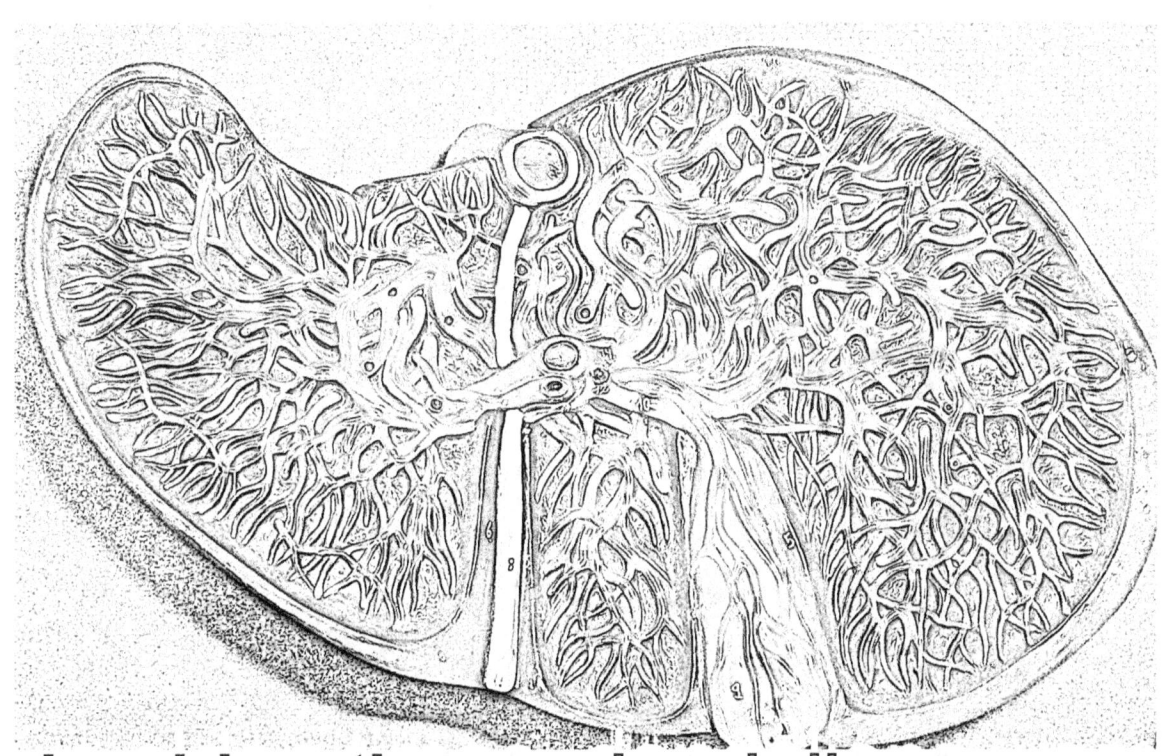

In olden times, dandelions were
prescribed for every ailment
from warts to the plague.

To this day, herbalists
hail the dandelion as
the perfect plant medicine
It is a gentle diuretic that
provides nutrients and
helps the digestive system
function at peak efficiency.

Dandelion leaves can shove their way though gravel and cement, and thrive in barren habitats.

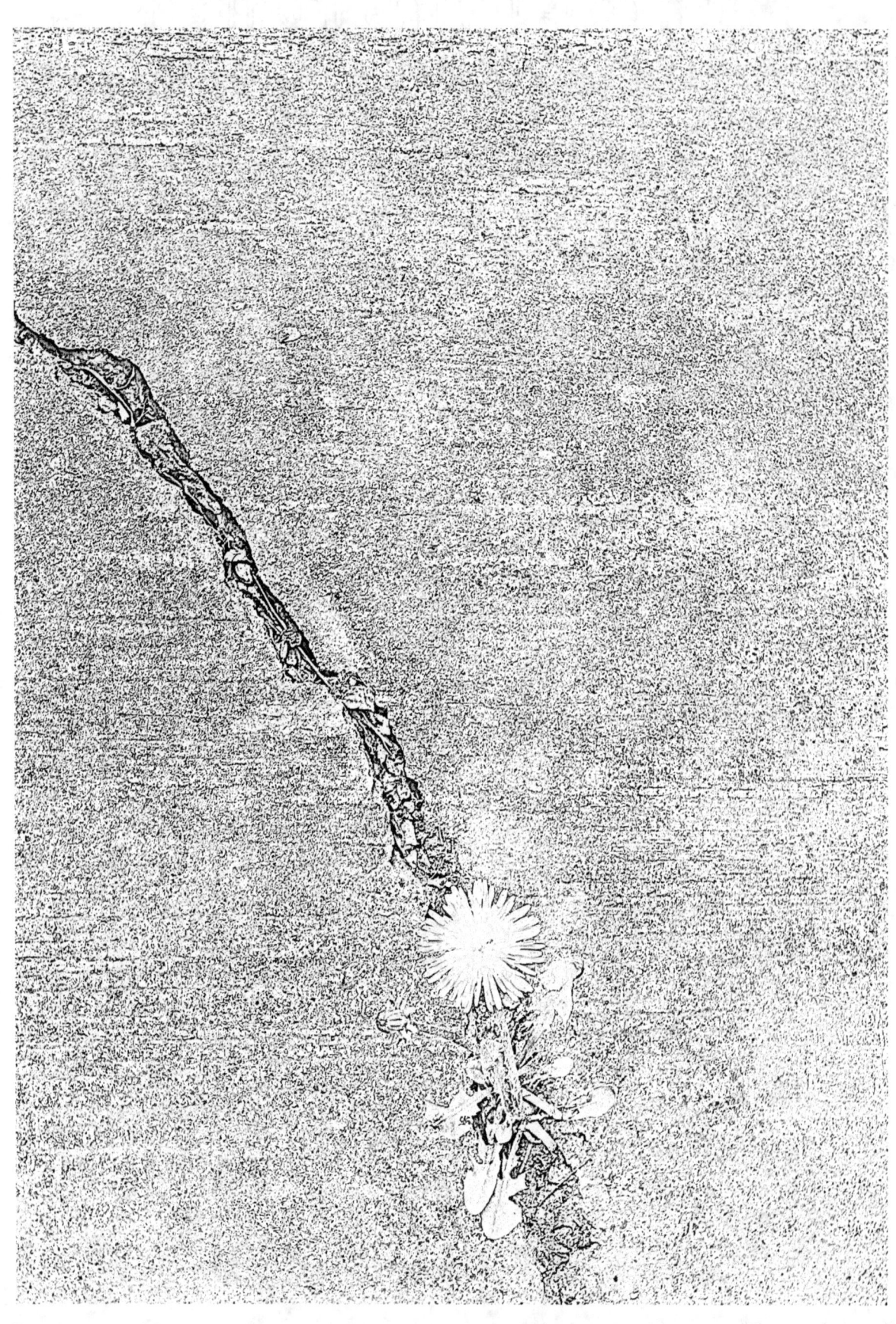

why is this plant so hard to kill?
dandelions are fast growers,
the cheerful little yellow flowers
go from bud to seed in days.

An individual plant can live for
years, so the dandelion
in a corner of the playground
might be older than the
children running past it.

The root can go down 15 feet.

A one-inch bit of dandelion root
can grow a whole new
dandelion.

For centuries, dandelions were the standard treatment for baldness, dandruff, toothache, sores, fevers, rotting gums, weakness, lethargy and depression:
all of them ailments caused by Vitamin deficiencies.

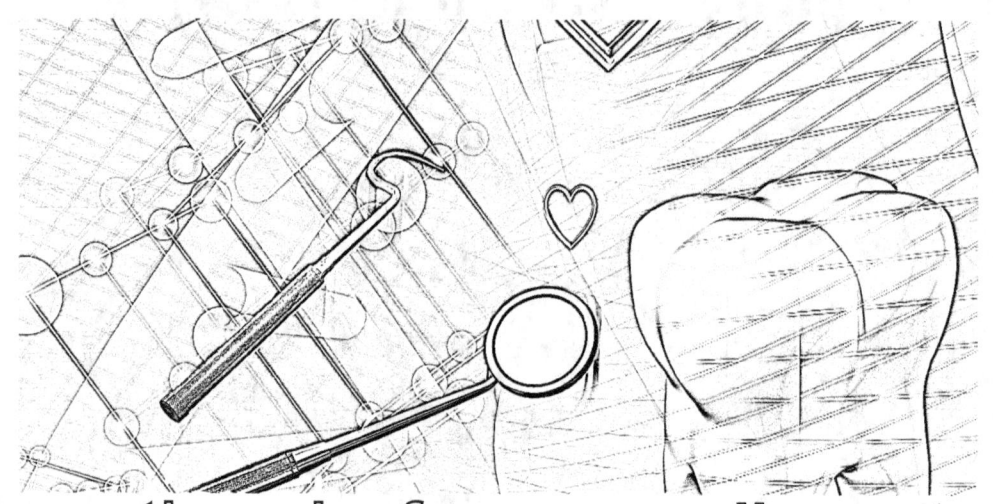

In a time before suppliments, vitamin deficiencies killed millions.

Data from the U.S. Department of Agriculture reveals:
They have more Vit A than spinach more vitamin C than tomatoes, and are a powerhouse of iron, calcium and potassium.

Dandelions require sun
and disturbed soil to thrive.
That's why they seem to
"look for" human activities
like roadsides, construction sites,
parking lots – and lawns.

Dandelions are masters of survival.

They can take root in places

that seem little short of miraculous,

and then are impossible to

get rid of, as homeowners
have found.

Dandelions are
good for your lawn.
Their wide-spreading roots
loosen hard-packed soil,
aerate the earth and help
reduce erosion.

The deep taproot pulls nutrients
such as calcium from deep in
the soil and makes them
available to other plants.

Dandelions actually
fertilize the grass.

There are a few dandelion
pretenders with yellow
ray florets that turn
into puffy seed heads
Just like the real thing.
Three of the most common are
catsears, hawkweeds
and hawksbeards.
You can confirm that a
dandelion is a REAL dandelion
by its unbranched, leafless,
hairless, hollow stems.

Why does it matter whether
a weed is a true dandelion?

Because if you
make a wish
and blow on
the seed head
of a false dandelion
your wish won't
come true.

The entire dandelion
plant is edible.

The dandelion
is also an
ingredient in
root beer.

Scientists created a new species of dandelion that produces high quality latex.

This type of latex has potential to replace rubber in the production of tires in the near future.

Sixty percent of the rubber consumed in the United States is used to make tires.
128 million scrap tires remain in stockpiles.

Some species of dandelion
live two years (biennial),
while others can survive longer
(perennial plants).

Dandelion is an herbaceous plant
that can reach
17 inches in height.
The stem is hollow.

Some people may develop
allergic reaction
(contact dermatitis)
after touching or
consuming dandelion.
The latex is a little caustic.
If you are allergic to the
regular variety of Latex,
you would probably react
to dandelions the same way.

Dandelions likely
originated
in Eurasia
30 million years ago.

Dandelion can be used
in the production of wine
and root beer.

Root of dandelion
can be used as a
substitute for coffee.

Dandelion flowers do not
need to be pollinated
to form seed.

What we think of as
the petals of a dandelion
flower are actually
individual flowers themselves.

They will produce fruit
called achenes,
followed by the tiny,
barbed brown seed
and it's accompanying
"parachute" that helps it
disperse in the wind.

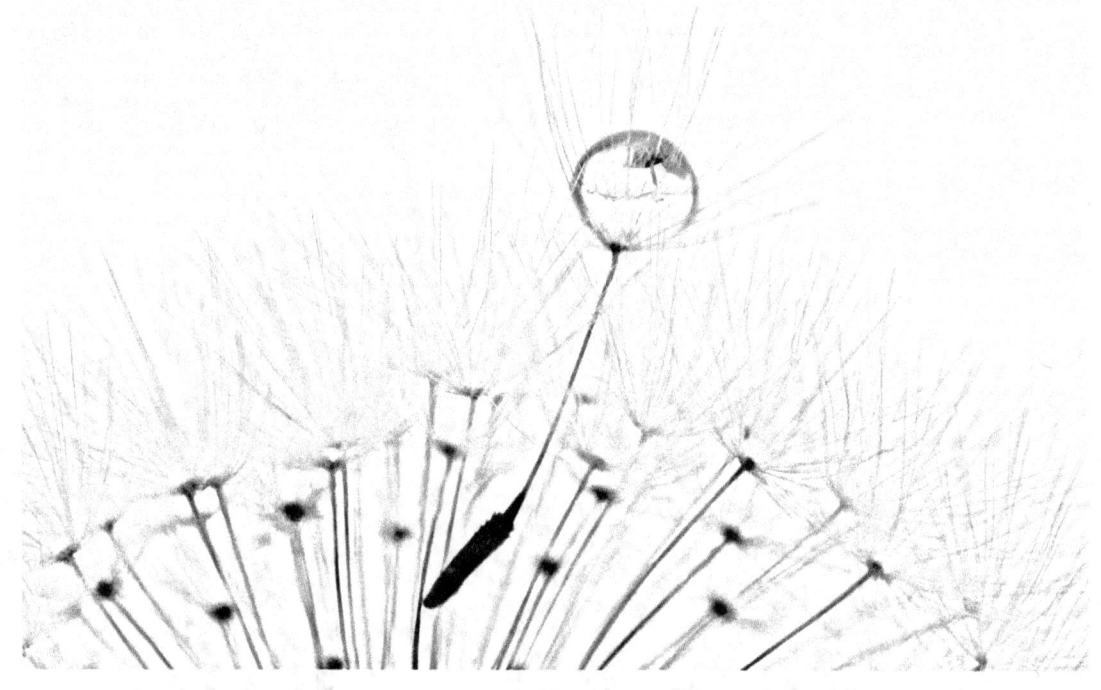

If you mow dandelions,
they'll grow shorter stalks
just to spite you!

Dandelions are
Dynamic Accumulators
that means they can draw
nutrients such as nitrogen
from the soil and concentrate
them in their leaves and roots.

Dandelions will produce
more seed than usual
if their habitat is disturbed
giving them a competitive edge
over other plants in the area.

Dandelions have a taproot
which can extend up to
a whopping 4.5 metres (15 feet)
underground, although you'll
typically find them top out
at 45 cm (18"), which is still
pretty long.

The taproot of dandelions
is very useful to
reduce compaction
in garden soil.

Dandelion flower heads
can be used to make
dye in the yellow-green
range.

The leaves will make
a purple dye.

Dandelion root is a stout, fusiform and fleshy taproot. Dark-brown on the outside with white pulp inside.

The root carries more bitter milky latex than the stems and leaves.

It's best to dig out the roots in the second year of the plants life.

In general, roots meant for medicinal purposes are harvested in summer and those used for drying and grinding to make coffee are harvested in autumn

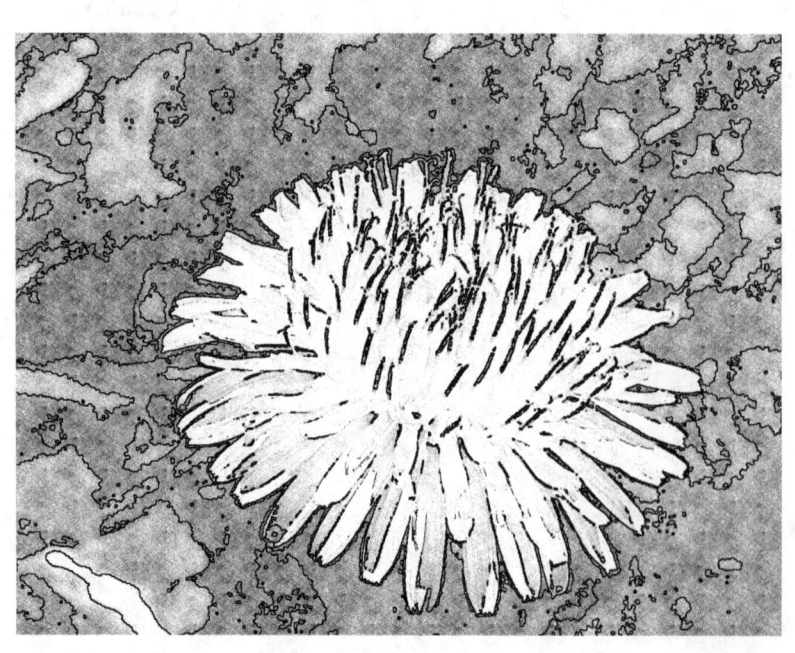

The root of dandelion cleanses the kidneys, gallbladder, liver, and lymph.

Therefore, it is also used in the treatments of numerous health issues, like gallstones, arthritis, constipation, rheumatism, hepatitis, acne and edema.

Dandelion root is extremely useful in the case of women's diseases, particularly in the prevention and treatment of numerous breasts issues, like cancer, cysts, tumors, and issues related to breast milk and breastfeeding.

Dandelion effectively detoxifies the liver, treats allergies, lowers cholesterol, stimulates the formation of bile, has diuretic properties, and is extremely useful for pregnant and postmenopausal women.

The dandelion stem purifies the blood, relieves stomach issues, regulates the metabolism and stimulates the gallbladder function.

DANDELION

Vitality

—

Empowerment

—

Perseverance

It is also used in folk medicine as a
powerful remedy against diabetes,
and the milk from the stem,
is very healing and is
used for removing warts.
Its flowers are used in the
preparation of dandelion syrup,
also known as honey,
which purifies the blood,
improves digestion,
and relieves a cough.

Spread the root on a flat surface,
in a cool dry place with
good air flow.
Leave the dandelion roots
to dry for 13-14 days.
As soon as they become
brittle under the fingers,
they are dry enough.
Then, store them in a jar,
and keep it in a dry,
dark place or up to a year.

Dandelion root tea- recipe:

Dry some dandelion leaves,
chop them finely and mince them.
Store them in a jar for future use.
Every day, add a ½ teaspoon
in a glass of water and
drink it regularly.

Dandelion tea recipe:

Dandelion tea recipe:

Mix 60 grams of the fresh dried leaves

30 grams of dried dandelion root with

2.5 ounces of water and a pinch of salt.

Bring the liquid to boil and cover the pan
let it simmer for 20 minutes.
Then, strain it and consume
three cups of this tea on a daily basis.

Dandelion syrup:

Pick 400 yellow dandelion flowers
pour 3 liters of cold water over
them.
Add 4 lemons and 4 oranges
cut in slices
leave the mixture for 24 hours.

Afterward, strain the mixture
through cheesecloth,
and transfer the resulting
liquid in a pot.
Add 2 cups of sugar and
cook for about
an hour and a half,
stirring frequently.

As soon as it boils,
and it is thick enough,
reduce the heat and
pour the hot syrup in hot,
sterilized jars.
This syrup is excellent for
treatment of a cough, cold,
bronchitis, and it is
safe for children.

Dandelion effectively detoxifies the liver, treats allergies, lowers cholesterol, stimulates the formation of bile, has diuretic properties, and is extremely useful for pregnant and postmenopausal women.

The dandelion stem purifies the blood, relieves stomach issues, regulates the metabolism and stimulates the gallbladder function.

It is also used in folk medicine as a
powerful remedy against diabetes,
and the milk from the stem,
is very healing and is
used for removing warts.
Its flowers are used in the
preparation of dandelion syrup,
also known as honey,
which purifies the blood,
improves digestion,
and relieves a cough.

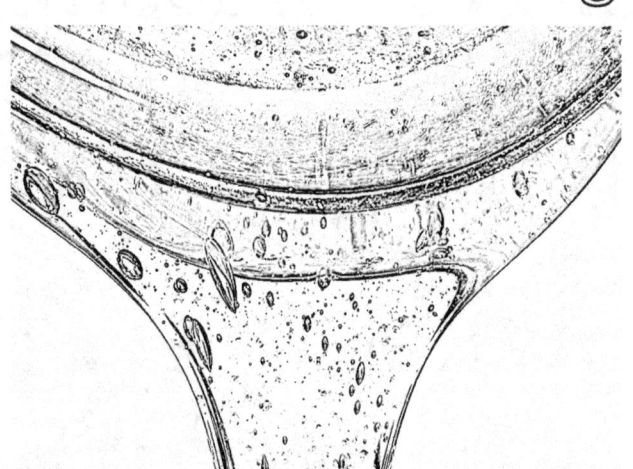

We've barely scratched the surface
of how awesome Dandelions are.
And you thought they were just weeds!!
For more Educational Coloring Books,
please Like The Author's
Facebook page.
www.Facebook.com/Kai Bantaign

www.ingramcontent.com/pod-product-compliance
Lightning Source LLC
Chambersburg PA
CBHW081153280526
45787CB00008B/3306